WONDER-FULL

Activate Your Inner Superpowers

D1532780

WONDER-FULL

Activate Your Inner Superpowers

(No
Cape
Required)

KELLY RADI

Edited by Angela Wiechmann

Graphics from Vecteezy.com

ISBN: 978-1-64343-931-0

Library of Congress Catalog Number: 2019905022

Printed in the United States of America

First Printing: 2019

23 22 21 20 19   5 4 3 2 1

Illustration and book design by Athena Currier

Beaver's Pond Press, Inc.

7108 Ohms Lane

Edina, MN 55439–2129

(952) 829-8818

www.BeaversPondPress.com

To order, visit www.ItascaBooks.com or call 1-800-901-3480 ext. 118.

Reseller discounts available.

Kelly Radi

www.raditowrite.com

To Brooke and Karen:

You amaze me with your resilience, grit, and grace.

Thank you for teaching me some of my greatest life lessons.

Praise for Wonder-Full

"Kelly shares actionable and powerful ideas to **step up your game at work and in life**. The simple tools can be implemented right away for quick impact. Plus, her inspiring stories are a joy to read."

—Kristen Brown, best-selling author of *The Happy Hour Effect* and *The Best / Worst Thing* and keynote speaker

"This book was **written with grace, gifts, and guts**. You will be taken on a journey that will ignite your inner strength and connect you to that little girl who believed she could conquer the world. I was engaged, encouraged, and educated through every chapter."

—Jennifer Lamb-Randolph, founder and president, i.V. Life

"What a treasure! As I read this, I felt myself nodding yes. Yes to authenticity and honesty. Yes to celebrating more and judging less. Yes to self-care and confidence. Yes to lifting each other up. Yes to the wonder and beauty within each person. This will be **a book we read and reread—a book we buy our daughters**."

—Annie Meehan, professional speaker and author of *Be the Exception*

"Kelly Radi is both a teacher and a storyteller. Following her journey from her life experiences, she gives the truths and powerful tools to live our own authentic lives. This is an **excellent book for recreating our lives and finding our own superpowers**."

—Dayna Deters, author of *Gluten-Free Momma Fit Cookbook* and
The Girl Who Created Her Own Happiness

"We are all Wonder Women in our own way, but sometimes we need someone to help us remember it. *Wonder-Full* is filled with humor, heartfelt stories, encouragement, and the space to write our own reminders to live our best life. **You won't be able to put this book down**, and you will come back to it over and over again. This will be one of your favorite books!"

—Kelly Sayre, founder and president, the Diamond Arrow Group

"A philosopher once said, 'Life is not a problem to be solved, but a reality to be experienced.' Kelly Radi's *Wonder-Full* guides us through what it means to persevere in the difficulties of real life challenges to truly live our lives in 'full.' **Get two copies—one for you and one for someone in your tribe!**"

—Mariellen Jacobs, founder, Rail Against the Danger

Contents

Introduction

What Would Wonder Woman Do?

When you think of a strong, smart, powerful woman, who comes to mind?

For me, the answer is simple: Wonder Woman. She's the original face of girl power.

Wonder Woman is the most popular female comic book superhero of all time. Through comics, cartoons, TV shows, and movies, she has been a role model for generations of girls. She proves women can be tough and smart and successful. She demonstrates they can be leaders—a revolutionary idea when she was introduced in the '40s.

My Wonder Woman obsession began in the '70s, when Lynda Carter masterfully portrayed this heroine on television. For each episode, I'd plop down on our shag rug and fire up our Zenith, which was the size of a VW Beetle, and enveloped in the finest mock-oak veneer.

I was always eager to see what superpowers and tools of the trade she would use to fight for truth and justice. Would it be her star-studded tiara? Her acute empathy? Her golden Lasso of Truth? Her magic bracelets? Would she run at super speed without tripping in her spectacular sky-high boots? (That in itself was a feat!)

While Wonder Woman's superpowers are impressive, I believe it is her strength of character that gives her true staying power. That's why I ask myself *What would Wonder Woman do?* whenever I face a challenge.

Wonder Woman is much more than just a superhero. Take it from the two women who have brought her to life: Lynda Carter and Gal Gadot.

Wonder Woman has helped transform how women and girls see themselves . . . she represents what we know is inside every one of us: fierce strength, a kind heart, and incredible valor.

— LYNDA CARTER

Wonder Woman, she's amazing. I love everything that she represents and everything that she stands for. She's all about love and compassion and truth and justice and equality, and she's a whole lot of woman.

— GAL GADOT

Wonder Woman has integrity. She does the right thing. Always. Even when it is difficult or embarrassing or unpopular. And even when nobody is looking.

She's authentic. She knows who she is and what she stands for. She faces challenges head on. Make no mistake about it: Wonder Woman takes action. She's resilient, never stopping until she accomplishes her mission.

And through it all, she has the heart of a woman.

She is Wonder-Full.

Real-Life Wonder Women

But let's get something clear right away: this isn't a book about Wonder Woman. It's a book about you, me, and all the other real-life Wonder Women out there.

It's a book about us, for us.

You and I are complex, just like Wonder Woman. Like her, we must balance the dichotomies of softness and toughness, compassion and grit, intelligence and instinct. She brings these powers to the Justice League. You bring them to the boardroom, dinner table, committee meeting, soccer game, blind date, and parent-teacher conference.

You have the same superpowers as Wonder Woman. Don't believe me? Check this out:

★ You may not have to wrestle a seven-foot-tall, five-hundred-pound gorilla to the ground, but you do wrestle with how to tactfully and effectively address your employee's or teenager's attitude.

★ You may not have to participate in a corrupt beauty pageant to untangle a web of sleazy enemy saboteurs, but you do untangle and silence the negative voices that try to sabotage your path to success.

★ You may not have the fate of the world resting on your ability to save the great minds of America from evil alien forces, but you do have the fate of your relationships resting on your ability to communicate, forgive, and set healthy boundaries.

★ You may not have to pull off a tightrope walk forty thousand feet in the air to stop nuclear warheads, but you do have to pull yourself up by your proverbial bootstraps when the going gets tough and your energy is depleted.

★ You may not have to help the police find a car theft ring and a Rolls-Royce with a valuable microchip hidden in its hood ornament, but you may have to help your best friend find her voice and value during a low point in her life.

Ladies, get ready to unleash your inner Wonder Woman. Let her inspire you to make decisions based on truth and authenticity. To lift up your fellow sisters. To be a woman of integrity.

Because you are Wonder-Full too.

The Seven Pillars of Power

Wonder Woman's colorful history is undeniably intertwined with the stories of Greek mythology, so it seems only fitting that we use pillars as a metaphor in this book.

In ancient Greek architecture, pillars provide structure, order, and beauty. In this book, you will learn about the Seven Pillars of Power that uphold and support you, as a woman. These pillars will help you grow personally, professionally, and relationally, and will empower you to live your life to the fullest.

1. The Power of Resilience

2. The Power of Authenticity

3. The Power of Priority

4. The Power of Tribe

5. The Power of Grace

6. The Power of Voice

7. The Power of Perspective

Like a woman, this book has serious parts, silly parts, raw parts, and reflective parts. It contains heartfelt stories, thought-provoking quotes, inspiration from Wonder Woman, and ample space to doodle and journal as you think about the Seven Pillars of Power and the superpowers you possess.

This is a thoughtbook, not a workbook. I hope you get what you need from it and can feel the love and passion I put into writing it. Please make it uniquely yours and use it to grow as a woman and to celebrate *you*.

Wonder-Full you.

No cape required.

The First Pillar of Power

THE POWER OF RESILIENCE

Falling Down

This is not how it's supposed to be, I thought as my husband and I packed up our daughter's belongings from her dorm room.

I choked back tears as I boxed up Karen's barely used Keurig and like-new textbooks, her fluffy white comforter and coordinating desk lamp. These items had been so full of promise and possibility when we helped her unpack them three short weeks earlier. Now they were painful reminders of how the best laid plans can change in the blink of an eye.

In a fluke accident two weeks into the school year, Karen sustained her third concussion. Her third traumatic brain injury. And at that moment, her collegiate path—and life as she knew it—was altered. We had to make the difficult decision to medically withdraw her from her first semester of college.

Karen had been through two concussions already, so we knew there was no Magic 8-Ball to tell us what to expect for recovery time. That's the thing about concussions: they affect each person differently. Sometimes people recover quickly, in a matter of a few days. Others, such as our daughter, are not so fortunate. She's one of the unlucky few who are more prone to receiving concussions and who require a much longer recovery. We couldn't predict whether her recovery would take weeks or months.

And to a kid who's eager to begin college and her next chapter in life, that feels like an eternity. Instead of living in the dorm and going to classes, she'd be spending the upcoming months living at home to allow her brain the time and the space it needed to heal. Instead of taking quizzes, ordering midnight pizzas, and attending football games, she'd be juggling a full calendar of occupational therapy, vision therapy, speech therapy, physical therapy, pain management, and most importantly, rest.

I struggled as a mom. Those of you who are also mothers know the powerful instinct to protect our offspring. We want to prevent or remove their pain and fear. And let me tell you, my baby girl was hurting and terrified. I didn't know what I could say or do to help her through this difficult season of her life. This was a problem I could not fix. I felt the urge to protect her, yet I was helpless.

She had to process her disappointment and overwhelming sadness. She needed time to mourn and time to heal—in more ways than one. This was a true test of resilience for her.

And for me.

Are You Resilient?

We all have times in our lives when we fall down—literally or figuratively—and find ourselves bruised emotionally, physically, or spiritually. What do you do when you fall? Do you stay down? Or do pick yourself back up? When you're faced with obstacles, stress, and other environmental threats, do you succumb? Or do you surmount?

What would Wonder Woman do?

Resilience in its simplest form is our ability to bounce back from adversity as efficiently as possible. Maybe you're recovering from a medical situation, like Karen. Maybe you're working in an adverse business setting. Maybe you're healing from a rough divorce or coming to terms with a personal loss or trauma. Whatever adversity you may be facing, resilience is the superpower that will keep you functioning—both physically and psychologically.

When you are resilient, you harness the inner strength that helps you rebound from a setback. Without resilience, you might dwell on problems too long, become overwhelmed, begin to feel victimized, or turn to unhealthy coping mechanisms.

Please understand, however, that resilience can't make your problems go away. Rather, it gives you the ability to see past them and work through them. It can improve your ability to cope. You too can persevere.

Becoming more resilient takes time and practice. It is a choice. It involves being self-aware and taking action. Fortunately, experts tell us resilience is something you can continue to develop throughout life.

Whether you are currently working through a stressful or traumatic situation, or whether you simply want to improve your resiliency, here are five ways to help you become more resilient.

Grab a Hand

When you fall, it's ultimately up to you to pick yourself back up. But that doesn't mean you have to do it entirely alone. So whenever you're down, be sure to look up—you might just see some hands reaching down, ready to help you to your feet. That's why it's important to build strong, healthy, positive relationships with people who support and accept you in both good times and bad. These are the superheroes in your life who will lift you up and remind you of your purpose and value even when you cannot see it. (Remember—even superheroes need helping hands from time to time. That's what the Justice League is all about.)

Be Intentional

You can't pick yourself up if you're in denial about being down. Don't ignore your problems. Instead, identify your problems and priorities. Figure out what you need to do and create a plan to do it. Be like Wonder Woman and take action! Although it can take time to recover from a major setback, traumatic life event, or major loss, know that your situation *will* improve if you work at it.

Set Realistic Goals

Recovering from a major setback is hard work, and it can feel overwhelming. So how do you eat an elephant? One bite at a time! Break your goals down into bite-size chunks by setting short-term goals with realistic timeframes. Keep in mind that small steps are still steps in the right direction. Celebrate your successes to help you stay positive and motivated.

Take Care of Yourself

Get plenty of sleep. Eat a healthy diet. Get up and move. Do something physical every day, especially when you are recovering from trauma. De-stress with yoga, meditation, guided imagery, or prayer. In addition, do something that gives you a sense of accomplishment and purpose every day. These things really do work, but you actually have to do them if you want to see results.

Remain Hopeful

You can't change the past, but you can always look toward the future. Instead of fixating on what you cannot change or what has already happened, focus on what you can do to move beyond it. Think about what it would feel like to flourish. Accepting and even anticipating change makes it easier to adapt and embrace new challenges with less anxiety.

Through the Storm

After packing up Karen's things that bleak September day, I worked through my own stages of grief during the three-hour drive home. I cried big, ugly tears. I prayed. I released my own fear and frustration, my sadness for Karen and her delayed dreams.

About halfway home, I heard a loud crack of thunder. The sky opened up with raindrops pelting my windshield so hard the wipers struggled to keep up. Moments later, though, the rain stopped, and the sun broke through with radiant beams of light bouncing off the dash.

For me, the sunshine after the storm symbolized hope and resilience. More importantly, it reminded me to be grateful. Grateful she was alive and that she would recover over time. Grateful we'd get some "bonus" months with her at home. Grateful for her committed, caring team of docs, nurses, and therapists. And oh-so grateful for our village—the friends and family who had reached out to her and to us, offering much-welcomed hugs, support, and sympathy.

I vowed to work through the emotions of this situation. I knew I had to think like Wonder Woman. I had to let go of the words *supposed to*. As in, *this is not how it's supposed to be.* I needed to focus on the present. I had to remember to be grateful and keep my priorities in check.

Holding tight to my own resilience, I encouraged Karen to do the same. I reminded her that the path from point A to point B is not always a straight, smooth line. On the road of life, there are plenty of potholes. And yes, sometimes we fall.

But that's okay. Because like it or not, we grow the most when we fall and pick ourselves back up. We learn who we are and whom we aspire to be. We discover our strengths and the people who matter.

Bouncing Back

I'm thrilled to tell you that Karen has mostly healed from this experience. The process wasn't easy, though. She started every day with an excruciating headache. She had to wear "super-cute" glasses (just like Diana Prince wore) that were actually special prism lenses designed to help her eyes, which struggled to focus.

She missed her social life. A lot. She felt isolated, not being able to read a book or look at a television or computer or an iPhone for weeks. She just wanted to feel and act like a "normal" eighteen-year-old. She wanted to hang out on SnapChat, drive a car, stay up late, or go to a concert with friends. But she couldn't.

Not at first, anyway.

But thanks to the power of resilience, she made it. She was able to return to school part-time for the second semester, and then she returned full-time the next fall. She is happily living life again.

Karen is a real-life Wonder Woman. She overcame the odds. She dug deep even when she was tired and hurting. She persevered. She showed true grit and resilience.

You too have the power to dig deep when faced with the potholes in life. One small step at a time. Remember to reach for a hand of support. Be intentional, and be sure to take care of yourself as you channel your inner superpower of resilience to overcome adversity.

You can persevere. Yes, you can!

Victim or Victor? How Do You Tell Your Story?

When something bad happens, we often replay the event over and over in our heads, like an old movie reel we cannot turn off. And of course, we're starring as the victim in that movie.

Ruminating on negative events is natural. But unfortunately, it will not help you heal. However, writing your thoughts down on paper might.

The practice of expressive writing has been proven to help people gain insight and perspective. It involves free writing continuously for twenty minutes about a particular issue or challenge, exploring your deepest thoughts and feelings around it.

So grab a pen and give it a try! It could be a game-changer for how you process negative situations and may even boost your resilience.

On the following pages, start by writing about the negative side of an experience, problem, or relationship. Then explore the positive aspects or outcomes of this adversity.

For example, you might begin by describing the negative aspects of a disagreement you had with a coworker. But then you might reflect on the positives—how some important issues are now out into the open and how you learned more about your coworker's point of view.

Keep in mind this writing is not meant to be a rough draft of your next novel, nor is it something you need to share with anybody else. The goal is to get your thoughts down on paper, not to create a masterpiece.

Give yourself the gift of twenty minutes to write, and see if it improves your narrative around a challenging aspect of your life. It might give you the perspective to see a new movie reel. And this time, you can star as the victor who can overcome this challenge.

THOUGHTBOOK

The Second Pillar of Power

THE POWER OF AUTHENTICITY

Insta-what?

"You're not on Instagram?" she said with a gasp. She promptly took my phone and created an account for me.

Just like that, my sweet friend Pamela instantly brought me into this make-believe world where nobody burns a turkey or wears ratty sweatpants. Heck, nobody even has a zit! This is a magical fairyland where everybody has shiny hair, does yoga on stand up paddle boards, and takes exotic vacations.

The sun always shines on Instagram. There are no cloudy days.

Initially, I hesitated to venture into this virtual village of carefully curated life events, but then I started following a few people I knew.

And then the voyeur in me started following several people I didn't know. While I may not know where my beautiful new Instafriends live or even what their real names are, I know their well-dressed kids and well-groomed dogs, and I know what the family ate photographed for dinner. I also know that they are passionate about shiplap (thanks, JoJo!) and overly invested in succulents and hot cocoa stations.

No Filter Needed

My first Instagram post was a picture I took of our girls in Hawaii.

Take that, Instagrammers, I thought. *See? We've been on a tropical vacation, too.*

Of course, I took this photo before I knew filters were even a thing. But with the sun setting over the South Pacific, who cares?

My second post was a pic with our friend Maxwell, after his basketball game. Fortunately, his sweet smile is brighter than the shine bouncing off my prominent forehead and the gray streak in my part, which I didn't know how to Insta-correct.

For my third post, I thought I'd get on the *look at my lovely, relaxing life* bandwagon and show how I spent an afternoon on my porch reading and sipping soda from a trendy blue-and-white paper straw. I think it took me ten minutes and forty tries to get the flowers, soda, straw, and book into the shot. By that time, I was too tired to figure out how to use a filter.

Look, I'm the worst with a camera. Like, really bad. I have zero confidence in the photography department. And it shows. My photo roll doesn't look carefully curated. It looks like a kindergartener's first handmade book: big heads, small bodies, random colors, and fuzzy lines. All the filters in the world cannot correct my clunky camera skills.

Here's another example: Last Easter, I tried to photograph an Insta-worthy display of our dinner table. I'd watched a lifestyle television show where the hostess—she looked like one of the Stepford Wives—suggested layering textures and colors to create the most "appealing tablescape." (Her words, not mine. I didn't even know *tablescape* was a word.)

So I pulled out my gauzy white tablecloth from the front hall closet and spread it out in its wrinkled glory. That's when I realized it probably shouldn't have gone through the dryer after last Easter, because now it was four inches shorter than our table. But time was of the essence, so I pushed forward. I'm no quitter! My mother-in-law would be arriving in an hour, and I wanted my impressive tablescape to knock her socks off.

I layered robin's egg blue chargers and our everyday white plates. (I was too time-crunched to dig out the wedding china.) Then I added tarnished silverware, cloth napkins, and little pastel egg cups. I tried to make place card holders from wine corks, which I'd seen on Pinterest. But I scrapped that idea when my ink smeared and it looked like I'd consumed all six bottles of wine the corks had come from. #PinterestFail.

The pièce de résistance was my centerpiece, a shabby-chic-meets-farmhouse style tray holding store-bought decorated eggs (they looked better than the ones I'd made), fresh yellow tulips in a Ball mason jar, and a bright-green moss-covered rabbit.

Yes, I was going for the wow factor with this tablescape. I had my layers. I had my textures. I had my colors. And I had about two minutes to capture this springtime masterpiece for my Instagram followers. All forty-six of them.

I grabbed my trusty iPhone and started snapping. Of course, the noontime sun was throwing shadows all over the place, making my too-short white tablecloth look gray and dingy. And no matter what angle I tried (and I tried plenty), it always looked like the rabbit was shooting tulips from its butt. No filter was going to correct this hot mess!

Capturing Authenticity

Since then, I've pretty much given up on developing my photography skills. Instead, I decided to bless and release the notion that I could ever be an effective photographer. And by extension, I blessed and released the notion that I need to impress others with a seemingly perfect Insta-life.

But then I found myself in a quandary. As I was working on my recent website upgrade, my web designer said he wanted "authentic and creative" photos of me that revealed my outgoing personality and reflected my inner Wonder Woman.

In other words, he wanted a miracle. Any photo I'd take of myself would leave me looking like my tablecloth—gray, dingy, and four inches too short.

Thankfully, my daughter Karen knows how to work a camera and edit photos like nobody's business. So I hired her as my official photographer. (And by hired, I mean I bought her lunch.)

Karen was so excited to hit the pavement and start shooting. I'm telling you, that kid had me feeling like a twenty-eight-year-old supermodel in no time!

For one pose, she had me sit down and lean over with my chin in my hands. It was the look-into-my-eyes-and-see-how-sweet-and-approachable-I-am money shot. It was great . . . in theory.

You see, when you pose for this shot and you are not, in fact, a twenty-eight-year-old supermodel but rather a forty-seven-year-old with thinning, crepey skin, you get mile-long cleavage that runs up to your neck.

When viewing this picture back at home on the computer, my first reaction was, "I need a new bra." My second was, "I'm trying to market my speaking services and books, not a peep show!"

"I can fix that!" Karen said.

And before you could say "Dolly Parton," my monster cleavage was gone, along with the rogue pimple that had sprouted earlier that day. The editing also removed some creases and lines, replacing them with more-luminous skin.

I remember thinking, *Does this qualify as "authentic and creative"? Is it possible to filter out the wrinkles of life yet still be authentically me?*

I decided the answer was yes. Photographs are not mirrors. Sometimes they distort reality, so it's okay to use a little editing to bring it back in. After all, it's not like all that editing made me look like a supermodel or an Insta-star trying to impress. It simply made me look like *me*. (Okay, a slightly spruced-up, "creative" version of me.)

And then the true moment of authenticity hit me as I looked over at my sweet baby girl. (No matter how old she gets, she'll always be my baby.) She was leaning over her computer, so eager and generous to share her time and talents to help me out with this project. She was focused. Honest. Vulnerable. Authentically her. And all I saw was sheer, radiant beauty.

This is real life, folks. No filters needed.

Authenticity in Business and in Life

So what makes a person authentic? Is it the ability to express yourself honestly and openly? Are you inauthentic when you filter photos? Does social media corrupt authenticity?

I think authenticity is bigger than social media and filters. I think it has to do with your character and your vulnerability. It's about being consistent with your words and deeds, regardless of circumstances. It's about being comfortable with who you are and owning your past, even if it's not so pretty.

In *Authentic: How to Be Yourself and Why It Matters*, psychologist Steven Joseph explains that authentic people know themselves. They can listen to their inner voice and can understand the complexities of their feelings.

By showing your true feelings, you allow others to know who you are and what you stand for. Authentic people are able to do this, and it frees them from the burden of bottled-up emotions.

In addition, being authentic allows us to feel accepted, understood, and valued in our relationships, which in turn allows us to drop our defenses. We naturally begin to examine ourselves psychologically, embrace new information, and live more authentically. What's more, studies report that authenticity leads to true happiness.

Leave it to research professor and *New York Times* bestselling author Dr. Brené Brown to summarize it so beautifully:

> **To be authentic, we must cultivate the courage to be imperfect—and vulnerable. We have to believe that we are fundamentally worthy of love and acceptance, just as we are. I've learned that there is no better way to invite more grace, gratitude and joy into our lives than by mindfully practicing authenticity.**

Authenticity is less about using filters and more about being brave. So friends, it is possible to be authentic and creative. Accepting and honest. Brave and vulnerable. Imperfectly beautiful.

(And it's okay to use an Instagram filter once in a while.)

So go forward and live your authentic life. Step up. Speak up. And live it up! Celebrate what makes you *you*. Watch as your thoughts, words, and actions influence the people around you in bolder, more positive ways.

Let your inner superhero shine!

How can you grow in authenticity? How can you make it a Pillar of Power that will serve you well?

Ask yourself, *What would Wonder Woman do?*

You already know she's a woman of strong moral character, so start there. Think about your character, your integrity. Be *you*! Be honest and trustworthy.

Authentic people don't just talk the talk. They walk the walk. As my friend, Dr. Jermaine Davis says, "Make sure your audio matches your video." Wonder Woman sure does! So back up your words with your actions.

And do you see Wonder Woman comparing herself to others? Feeling small? Second guessing her good works? I don't think so!

If she doesn't do these things, then you don't need to either. What purpose does comparison serve? You are uniquely you. You have your own strengths, your own weaknesses, and your own path to happiness and success. So focus on *your* super-powers and *your* aspirations.

On my path to authenticity, I had to bless and release my unrealistic desire to capture and create an Insta-worthy life. What (or who) can you bless and release today to allow yourself to grow in authenticity?

THOUGHTBOOK

The Third Pillar of Power

THE POWER OF PRIORITY

Multitasking and Motherhood

Our friends have one-year-old twins, a boy and a girl. William and Elin are adorable and busy, as babies tend to be. Their mom, Carrie, juggles the demands of motherhood, work, and marriage like a champ. Her kiddos are well-dressed, well-fed, and deeply loved. And she still finds time to post precious baby pics on her Instagram feed so the rest of us can enjoy the little cherubs too.

Young moms such as Carrie are especially famous for this type of juggling act. They can breastfeed, respond to emails, apply mascara, and write up a grocery list—all at the same time.

I may be beyond those baby-rearing years, but I remember the gerbil wheel of young motherhood. I remember the funky-sweet scent of bleach-meets-spit-up, the endless loads of laundry, the sticky kitchen floors, and the even stickier kisses. I remember yearning for a day when my house would be clean and presentable, when I could walk from one end to the other without stepping on a Lego or a Matchbox car or a plastic banana.

I remember dreaming of having my own Alice. You know, the lovable live-in housekeeper from *The Brady Bunch*—the one in the blue dress and pristine white apron. My Alice would have Palmolive-soft hands from doing all my dishes. She'd make me coffee and roast turkey and greet me with a smile and a spotless kitchen every morning. Alice would make my life groovy! She'd handle the daily grind so I could just enjoy my kids. It was a fabulous dream!

But reality prevailed. I had no Alice. Instead, I learned how to juggle my own responsibilities. I'll try not to brag, but I developed some mad multitasking skills. In the time it took to brush my teeth, I could make the bed, change a load of laundry, listen to the morning news on the radio, take out the trash, and clip my toenails.

My multitasking prowess only grew stronger as the girls grew older. After all, this was what motherhood was all about, right? Why do one thing when you could do five things—or more—all at the same time?

So Many Yeses—So Little Time

And of course, why would I stop at juggling just my family commitments? Why not throw some professional and community commitments into the mix too?

"Kelly, will you direct the Sunday school Christmas pageant?"

Yes.

"Can you run the Girl Scout booth at the next event?"

Yes.

"Kelly, you're a writer. Will you please review and edit my resumé?"

Yes.

"Can you cover a shift this weekend?"

Yes.

"Will you organize this fundraiser?"

Yes.

So many yeses. Can you relate? They were all for good causes. But they were no good for me or my family.

I found myself snapping at my husband for no apparent reason and getting short with my kids.

They just don't get it, I thought. *They don't understand how much I do.*

Instead of resembling *Better Homes & Gardens*, our once-tidy house started looking like a scene from *Hoarding: Buried Alive*.

No time to clean, I thought.

I stopped doing my daily devotions.

No time for that either, I thought. *God will understand.*

At one point, I took great pleasure in making my signature home-cooked meals. But now I took shortcuts in the kitchen wherever I could. Forget homemade pot pies. It's freezer-to-oven fish sticks for you little buggers!

Cooking takes energy I just don't have right now, I thought.

The illusion of multitasking gave way. I once prided myself on being able to talk on the phone while responding to emails. Suddenly, I realized I was only half listening to the phone conversations and forgetting to add proper attachments to the emails. I was lost in space between the two tasks. I couldn't get my overstretched brain to think clearly.

Multitasking and Marijuana

I swear—I wasn't smoking anything. But I might as well have been.

Research from the Institute of Psychiatry at the University of London shows that workers distracted by emails and phone calls had a ten-point drop in IQ, which is more than twice the effect of smoking marijuana. Seriously, multitasking is worse than doing dope.

Multitasking is a trick we play on ourselves. We think we're getting more done. In reality, it slows our productivity and our brain power. Our productivity drops as much as 40 percent.

It's not multitasking but actually *switch* tasking. We force our brains to rapidly shift from one thing to another, which only interrupts our thought patterns. Each switch makes us lose time and productivity in the process.

When I first read those multitasking studies, I figured I was different—I had to be the exception. Maybe multitasking made *other* people lose productivity. But not *me*. After all, I'd done it for so many years and I was very good at it. Practice, I thought, had made me the perfect multi-taskmaster.

But I was wrong. In my quest to quickly tick all the boxes on my lengthy to-do lists, I became less competent and less detail oriented. In fact, studies show that those of us who think we're especially good at multitasking have a harder time switching tasks than people who usually don't multitask at all.

More importantly, I realized that multitasking made me less *present* in my tasks and my life. I was no longer paying attention to conversations. I was no longer fully engaged with my family or friends.

It made me forget what was important.

One evening, my daughter said, "Mom, even when you're here, you're just not *here*. I miss talking with you."

Ouch.

From the mouth of a babe (or in this case, a teen) came the words I needed to hear. I realized that doing it all at once was not always a good thing. My intentions were pure but somehow skewed.

Maybe those scientific researchers had a point about multitasking.

Maybe I needed to reevaluate my ideas of efficiency. I had to take a close look at my priorities and recognize that time is not an unlimited commodity.

Maybe I just had to do less better.

P Is for Priorities and Presence

Do less better. What a concept!

Doing less better is about reducing pressure and gaining margin. It means putting your precious energy into fewer areas so you can do them well. It means not taking on too many projects and doing them poorly—and feeling bad about it the entire time.

It's about learning to say no to the excessive or unnecessary commitments that drain your tank so you can say yes to those that fill it. For example, it could be saying no to yet another church committee or business opportunity so you can sit down to dinner without your phone in front of your face. It might mean giving yourself permission to blow off laundry to play a board game or read a book or phone a friend. It might mean a night of binge-watching old episodes of *The Desperate Housewives*, just because.

On a deeper level, though, it may mean letting go of the preconceived notion that you're not a "good mom" if you don't attend every school fundraiser or that you're not a "good employee" if you decline a networking event. It might even mean letting go of the idea that you're not a superhero if you can't take on everything in the world at once.

Do you think Wonder Woman ever needs to reevaluate her to-do list? I do. She is, after all, a woman. Like all of us, she plays many roles and carries many responsibilities. In fact, her alter ego is Diana Prince, a working woman who has worn many hats over the years, including US Army nurse, military intelligence officer, businesswoman, astronaut, and staff member at the United Nations. Like us, she has to continually evaluate her commitments to make sure her priorities align with her values.

And it doesn't make her any less Wonder-Full.

How Priorities Lead to Presence

Here's what I did when I decided to do less better: I called upon the power of priority.

I used to start my days with an unrealistic, overscheduled calendar and overflowing to-do lists. That was a recipe for disaster. It kept me from feeling productive or having balance between my work and life commitments.

Now I prioritize. I pick three—only three—work projects to complete in any given day. It's kinda like the combo meal at a Chinese buffet, where you pick three entrees to go with your fried rice. Like choosing cream cheese wontons, orange chicken, and beef with broccoli, I choose three tasks to fill my plate. (General Tso's will have to wait for another day, no matter how tasty it looks.)

On top of that, I then focus on one task at a time before moving on to the next. That's like finishing the wontons first, then the orange chicken, then the beef with broccoli. If you try to scarf it all down at once, you can't savor the flavors—and you might just end up needing the Heimlich.

As a speaker and writer, a typical day might see me writing a blog, practicing a presentation, and making calls to potential clients. By turning off my phone while I'm practicing and not answering emails when I'm writing, I am more engaged, more efficient, and much more productive. And by focusing on one task at a time, I get to honor the process and actually enjoy my work. I'm more present in many ways.

Don't get me wrong. Prioritizing doesn't magically make your responsibilities go away. I still don't have an Alice, so there's laundry to fold and dishes to do. I still have more tasks than time.

But now I tackle them with a different attitude and fortitude. Gone are the days of reducing brain power with endless multitasking. (I don't know where you're at in your life, but I'm currently in the perimenopausal season, and I need all the brain power I can muster.)

And thanks to prioritizing, I now know how to take—to savor—those golden opportunities to talk with one of my kids or join friends for happy hour. I don't waste the precious good stuff by checking emails or Facebook. I choose to be in the moment—without distractions.

I choose to be present.

Take some time today to think about your life . . . your commitments . . . your priorities. Do they align?

★ What fills your tank?

★ What depletes it?

★ Do you have margin?

★ How can you slow down, reprioritize, and do less better?

★ How can you be more present in your life?

Pick Three (Just Like the Chinese Buffet!)

Try this experiment: For the next week, prioritize your to-do lists. Pick three—only three—significant tasks or projects to complete each day. Remember to complete each task before going on to the next.

Day #1
MY THREE PRIORITIES

Day #2
MY THREE PRIORITIES

Day #3
MY THREE PRIORITIES

Day #4

MY THREE PRIORITIES

Day #5

MY THREE PRIORITIES

Day #6

MY THREE PRIORITIES

Day #7

MY THREE PRIORITIES

Does this help you focus? Increase productivity? Allow you to unplug once you've completed the tasks? Are you more present?

THOUGHTBOOK

The Fourth Pillar of Power

THE POWER OF TRIBE

Legend tells us that before she was Wonder Woman, she was Diana, the Amazon princess. She lived on a lush island paradise called Themyscira, where she was raised by a community of women. They were her tribe. They believed in her, guided her, and honored her—even when she left the island for the modern world. While Wonder Woman was certainly gifted with many superhuman powers, I believe the support of these women was one of her greatest sources of strength.

You don't have to be an Amazon to tap into the power of your own tribe. The people we choose to surround ourselves with can be incredible sources of strength and success. It's been said that you are the average of the five people you spend the most time with. Are you using your time wisely?

My Tribe

I had my own tribe as a young girl. I grew up in a small rural Midwestern town, where I was blessed to have both of my grandmothers, three great-grandmothers, and several aunts and great-aunts living in the community. Between my own mother and these extended family members, I was literally surrounded by women who wanted the best for me.

They taught me, corrected me, prayed for me, disciplined me, supported me, and loved me—no matter what. They were a positive, present force, encouraging me to make wise decisions and to work hard. Whatever I did, wherever I went, I knew they'd always have my back.

Like Wonder Woman's tribe, my tribe supported me as I left our small village for the "modern world." In my case, the modern world was my college town of Grand Forks, North Dakota. As I began my journey into adulthood, these women instilled confidence and values. They sent cookies and funny Hallmark cards.

And they didn't stop with North Dakota. They prayed for my safety as I moved to Memphis for my first "real" job after college. And still they sent cookies.

They later showered me with love, linens, and lingerie at a bridal shower in our church basement. (Grandma Esther gave me lingerie and told me to have fun with it!) And then these generous, caring women welcomed the next generation to the tribe when our daughters, Brooke and Karen, were born.

Even though some of these remarkable women have since passed away and moved on to a new kind of paradise, I still feel the foundation of support they laid for me. They continue to be a strong force in my life by the legacy they have left behind.

Because of what my original tribe taught me, I knew I needed to create a tribe wherever I lived. And I did. I found a circle of sisters in Grand Forks, another in Memphis, and yet another when I moved to a new community as a young bride.

These women are still my lifeline. Together, we've experienced potty training and puberty, job promotions and retirements, breast cancer and hot flashes, wrinkles and hair dye, regrets and pleasures, graduations and college, deaths of parents and births of grandchildren, divorces and weddings, heartaches and love. We know when to call an impromptu happy hour and who needs it most.

We push each other to be better. That's what tribes do. We encourage. We forgive. We celebrate successes with champagne. We face losses with grace—and lots of hugs. It's not a "me" mentality, but a "we" mentality. For better or worse, we are here to support one another.

Your Tribe

Ladies, if you want to see yourself and your future, take a close look at your friends. Who is in your tribe? Do you lift one another up? Do you push one another to be better? Or do you compare and judge one another? Do your values align?

If these questions revealed some issues about your tribe, you may want to make some changes. You may need to prune your friendship tree. You simply cannot function to your fullest potential by spending time with people who don't have your back.

As Matthew Kelly states in *The Rhythm of Life*:

> *The people we surround ourselves with either raise or lower our standards. They either help us to become the best version of ourselves or encourage us to become lesser versions of ourselves. We become like our friends. No man becomes great on his own. No woman becomes great on her own. The people around them help to make them great. We all need people in our lives who raise our standards, remind us of our essential purpose, and challenge us to become the best version of ourselves.*

The good news is that *you* have the power to choose your tribe. So do it! Reach out to women of integrity who aren't afraid to be vulnerable. Think about the kinds of people you want to surround yourself with:

★ The Inspired

★ The Honest

★ The Motivated

★ The Passionate

★ The Kind

★ The Grateful

★ The Open-Minded

Connect with women who truly want to support one another through the ups and downs of life. These sisters will be some of your greatest sources of strength and help you become the very best version of yourself.

Who is in your inner circle? List some of the people in your tribe.

★ _____

★ _____

★ _____

★ _____

★ _____

★ _____

Next, think about the reasons *why* you've chosen them for your tribe.

★ What makes them good friends or colleagues?

★ What makes them honorable women?

★ What attributes do they possess that you admire?

★ How do you support them?

THOUGHTBOOK

The Fifth Pillar of Power

THE POWER OF GRACE

I was overwhelmed. Tired. Depleted—physically and emotionally. I knew in my gut something had to give. But what?

How did I end up in that place, exhausted, broken, and in serious need of some grace?

Well, it began when our youngest daughter was heading to college and we were facing the empty nest. I decided to add a part-time position to my already busy life as a wife, mother, author, and speaker.

It worked for a while.

I loved my job as a volunteer coordinator for a hospice house. I had an incredible connection with my coworkers and the organization's volunteers. Linda, my boss, was phenomenal.

Plus, the busyness made me feel useful, intelligent, and valued. You've heard the old phrase: "Busy people get stuff done."

The Breaking Point

So, there I was, getting all kinds of stuff done. But then something changed within me. I'm not sure why, exactly.

Maybe it was because I landed several new speaking clients yet had to negotiate their contracts at ten thirty at night because it was my only free time. Maybe it was because of that terrifying drive to the ER after our daughter blacked out following her third concussion. Or because we had to move her things home from her dorm room three short weeks into her freshman year. Maybe it was because I was dealing with some ongoing extended-family drama and trauma. Or because I had stopped working out. Maybe it was because I no longer had time for the occasional happy hour or lunch date with my girlfriends.

All I know is that busyness stopped working for me about six months after I accepted the position. This went beyond setting daily priorities and being present, as the third Pillar of Power discusses. Something deeper was happening here.

I am a type A personality who strives for optimal results in all areas of my life. But at that moment, I wasn't bringing my A game to any of it. Worst yet, I was only hurting myself in this desperate attempt to balance it all.

Yes, something had to give . . . and I knew what that was.

The Drama and the Decision

Should I—could I—really quit my job?

Friends, you need to know I labored over this decision. I lost sleep over it. I cried big, wet elephant tears. Oh, the drama! If only you could have heard the voices arguing back and forth in my head like a bad soap opera scene.

Quit? What are you talking about? You love it there! Your work matters. You are touching lives.

Yes, but your husband misses you. You're failing him. You're never home.

Seriously, why would you quit an amazing job such as this? You get paid *to help people. It's fulfilling! Most people would give anything for that kind of job. Not to mention it gives you a steady paycheck, which you could use right now, you know?*

Yes, but your daughter is hurting. She needs you right now. #momfail

Your coworkers and volunteers are so sweet. How could you possibly bail on them?

Yes, but you need to focus on your writing and speaking. You don't have time and energy to get your next book done. Do you want to be a one-hit wonder, never to be published again? And do you want your speaking business to fail, or do you want to see it grow to its potential?

How could you even think of doing this to Linda? You've only been there seven months. She'll be so disappointed. She'll have to start the dreaded search for a new employee. You'll make a lot of extra work for her. And heaven knows she already has enough to do!

Yes, but—

C'mon, you can keep doing it all. It's what you do, *right?*

Each voice was loud and dramatic, and each seemingly had a point. I had to decipher which voice spoke my truth and which voice was merely pushing me deeper and deeper into this rut.

I needed the strength to make a difficult choice. I had to take action.

I had to quit.

Lessons from Linda

I anxiously scheduled a meeting with Linda so I could drop the bomb no hardworking non-profit director wants to receive from a valued employee.

"I need to quit," I blurted before I even sat down.

Boom.

Linda's response was not what you'd expect from a typical employer. But this woman is anything but typical.

She didn't say a word. Rather, she looked me in the eye and gave me space to speak. She listened carefully as the words came spewing from my mouth, like a faucet I couldn't turn off.

"You see," I hastily explained, "I love this job. And I hate to disappoint you. But my speaking career is taking off beyond my wildest expectations. And our daughter is home from college on a medical withdrawal. She really needs me to be present. I guess what I'm saying is, I simply can't manage all my responsibilities. I can't give the proper time and attention to my commitments, including my marriage and this job."

When I finally took a breath, Linda nodded.

"I accept your resignation," she said calmly.

But she didn't end the meeting to go handle her lengthy list of daily responsibilities—to which I had just added. Instead, this real-life Wonder Woman stayed and blanketed me in grace.

True grace.

Heartfelt grace.

She told me how much she appreciated my service. She affirmed the work I had done and what I had brought to the organization's culture. She said I'd be dearly missed by staff, clients, and volunteers. She even recognized and praised my work outside the office—my speaking and writing career and my volunteer activities.

And then this caring and insightful superhero asked if she could offer some personal advice.

Shocked, I nodded.

"Be kind to Kelly," she said.

With those four words, my lower lip started to quiver.

"You've been through a lot this year, and you're good at putting others' needs before your own," she continued. "But please give yourself permission to take care of *you*. Give yourself some grace. Just be kind to Kelly."

See? I told you she was phenomenal.

In the short time I worked under this woman, I learned so much about leading with kindness and grace. She taught me about prioritizing family and faith. She modeled what it meant to just be present. To listen without judgement. To love. To care.

As I prepared to leave, Linda offered me one more precious nugget of wisdom.

"It's okay to say no, even to good things."

Boundaries

What Linda meant was that setting boundaries is a valuable and healthy strategy. You need to set boundaries on the precious nonrenewable resource that is you—your time, your treasure, your talent, your totality. After all, you can't respect, protect, or be kind to yourself if you don't make decisions based on what is good for your own well-being.

While some folks in your life may push back at the boundaries you set for yourself, you'll discover that some people, such as Linda, are surprisingly respectful and responsive to them. They get it! Like you, they are seeking margin, space, and clarity.

These people are the diamonds. True treasures. Even if you tell them no or even if you give them your resignation notice, they'll continue to cheer for you along the way.

If you're lucky, you'll have Lindas in your life. With compassion and grace, they'll reinforce your core values and remind you when you're falling short of where you need to be. And just maybe they'll remind you when you need to be kind to yourself.

Listen to your Lindas, my friends. Give grace to one another. But also please know when and how to extend that same grace to yourself.

You are worthy.

Observe, without judgment, the conflicting voices in your head—the ones telling you what you should or shouldn't be doing. Where are these messages coming from? Guilt? Responsibility? Validation? Loyalty? Kindness? Busyness? Ego? Are they truths? Or are they stories you are choosing to tell yourself? Draw a picture or journal your thoughts about these messages.

Your thoughts have tremendous power. If you change the narrative in your head, you can change the trajectory of your life.

—KELLY RADI

Put your hand on your heart and read aloud this affirmation from *A Quiet Strong Voice* by Lee Horbachewski:

> *I allow myself to set healthy boundaries. To say no to what does not align with my values, to say yes to what does. Boundaries assist me to remain healthy, honest and living a life that is true to me.*

Now, what boundaries can you put into place today as the first step to being kind to yourself?

The Sixth Pillar of Power

THE POWER OF VOICE

Powerless or Powerful?

I was fresh out of college and twenty-two years-old—equal parts eager and naive. Thrilled to accept my first postcollege job as a dispatcher at a regional airline, I packed up my meager possessions and my Midwest work ethic and moved across the country. I learned the job quickly and worked hard to earn the respect of my mostly male peers.

The vice president of the airline even seemed impressed by my work. He'd go out of his way to speak with me, frequently stopping by my desk to check in and ask how things were going.

At first, I was flattered. Who wouldn't want to be noticed by the VP?

But soon I became uncomfortable. Initially, I couldn't quite put my finger on why. Then I started to notice how he lingered a little too long at my desk. And occasionally, I'd feel his eyes wander.

This married, middle-aged father of two young boys would tell inappropriate jokes—often at my expense. And often about female body parts. I'd nervously laugh to not stand out for being uptight. I'd heard watercooler conversations about former female employees who "couldn't take a joke." I didn't want any negative labels in the way of my promising aviation career.

So I chose to stay silent, despite the uneasy feeling that seemed to wash over me every time he walked into the room. Before long, I began to feel powerless, nervous, and scared.

One day while I was making copies in the back room, he walked in. Immediately, the hair on the back of my neck stood up. Without a word, he slithered up behind me. And before I even knew what was happening, he rubbed up against me and tried to stick his hand up my skirt. I froze.

But only for a moment.

Then I elbowed him in the ribs. I shouted his name, hoping it was loud enough for some-one else to hear, and then I followed it with, *"Get your hands off me! Don't ever touch me again!"*

At that moment, I chose to use my voice to send a powerful message to this man. And from that day forward, he never laid a hand on me again.

I went from feeling powerless, silent, and scared to standing up for myself. I took my power back. And I did it with my voice.

Becoming Wonder-Full

It wasn't easy, but through that awful situation many years ago, I grew. I discovered who I was and what I stood for. I identified the woman I wanted to be.

I wanted to be a woman who stood for truth and did the right thing even when it was difficult or embarrassing. And trust me when I say it is really embarrassing to be groped by your boss in the copy room. I also wanted to be a woman who did the right thing even when nobody was looking. And most of the time, doing the right thing means saying the right thing loudly enough to be heard.

When I look back at this time of my life, I realize I wanted to be like Wonder Woman. She's strong and always does the right thing, even when it's difficult and especially when nobody is looking.

From Mom to Spokesmom

I did eventually leave that job when I moved back to Minnesota to marry the love of my life. At that time, I left the aviation field and started working as a public relations account executive.

Then something wonderful happened: I became pregnant! After careful thought and consideration, I chose to leave the corporate world to become an at-home mom. It was a bold move and definitely a risk, but I was all in. I'm generally not the person who just dips her toes into the water. If I'm committed, I dive into the deep end head first! So I dove in and immersed myself in this new position of "mom."

With that decision, my signature scent went from Estée Lauder's Beautiful to spit-up! My professional look went from *Dynasty*-style suits and big hair to sweatpants and ponytails. Instead of setting up client meetings and coordinating video shoots, I was orchestrating playdates and watching Barney the dinosaur waddle around on TV. (Those of you who raised kids in that era are already cursing me, because you now have the Barney theme song chirping in your head: *I love you . . . you love me . . . we're a happy family . . .)*

While I was embracing my years of diaper duty, kissing boo-boos, and attending PTO meetings, changes were happening in the business world. This new thing called the internet launched. Before long, flash drives replaced floppy disks. Wi-Fi wasn't just sci-fi. The iPhone and social media were born. "B2B" and "B2C" became catchphrases. And of course, my beloved business suits with mile-high shoulder pads evolved into business casual.

About the time our firstborn hit her teens, I started getting itchy for a career change. I'd given my heart and soul to raising our girls and had no regrets. None. Yet I knew it was time for me to get back out there.

But how? I'd been out of the aviation industry for nearly two decades, and I hadn't pitched to a client, filled out an expense report, or written a press release for fifteen years.

There I was, an at-home mom with rusty skills. And let's just say there was no way I could still fit into my old business suits, even if they were in style (which they *weren't*). But I started putting feelers out anyway.

Then I hit the jackpot. I was offered a job that capitalized on my public relations degree while actually celebrating my mothering experiences. I would be a "spokesmom" for a family wellness initiative at a healthcare system.

A *spokesmom*. I'm not kidding! The job was perfect. I could use my experience, my voice, as both a mom and a professional. What a great way to step into my power!

Which Voices Do You Listen To?

I eagerly signed my employment contract on the dotted line. I would start in three weeks. Apparently, though, three weeks was too much time to think!

As eager as I had been at first, I became anxious. Petrified, actually. I'd wake up at night with nasty voices in my head.

You're too old to do this job.

Your skills are out of date.

You're not smart enough.

Hey, frumpy lady—you're not professional enough.

The clincher was the voice that told me, *You're just an at-home mom. You're not worthy of the position.*

Brutal, right?

Does this ever happen to you? Do you ever have those nasty voices tearing you apart? Stripping you of your confidence?

My husband and daughters could see the internal battle I was fighting with the voices. So the night before my first day of work, Marty and the girls sat me down at the kitchen table to give me a pep talk. I looked into their shiny blue eyes as they wrapped me in words of affirmation.

"You're going to be awesome!"

"You can do it."

"They are lucky to have you."

"We're so proud of you, Mom."

"You've got what it takes, Kel," Marty said. "Everybody knows this but you."

Marty and the girls then excitedly handed me a present. I carefully removed the crinkly tissue paper from the gift bag to reveal a vintage-inspired metal Wonder Woman lunchbox.

"Mommy, you're *our* Wonder Woman," Karen said with a grin.

As you can imagine, the lunchbox—and their words—brought me to tears. These voices of confidence and support were *real*. They replaced those negative voices in my head. Instead of thinking I was "out of date" or "dumb," my family believed I was smart and capable. And I knew—at that very moment—I needed to model those positive qualities for my girls.

I've since moved on from that job too. But in case you're wondering, that Wonder Woman lunchbox still sits on a shelf in my office as a daily reminder of why I do what I do. Somehow that hunk of tin helps me unleash my inner Wonder Woman. It reminds me I'm capable—silencing the negative voices that tell me I'm not enough.

It reminds me of the day my family taught me the true power of voice.

YOU HAVE A VOICE. YOUR WORDS MATTER.

You can use your voice to **take power back**, as I did with the inappropriate boss. You can use your words to **inspire others** and **help them find their own power**, as my family did for me. You can use your words to **drown out the negative voices** in your head.

Your words have power. **How are you using them?**

Use your voice to wrap yourself with words of affirmation. Start by listing five positive things about yourself.

1 _____
_____
_____

2 _____
_____
_____

3 _____
_____
_____

4 _____
_____
_____

5 _____
_____
_____

Now, speak these affirmations out loud, allowing them to sink in. Be bold! Be loud! Let your voice resonate and replace the negative voices.

Finally, end by saying these words, whether you shout them from a literal rooftop or whisper them in a moment of peaceful solitude. These are your words of power.

I am enough. I am capable. I am awesome.

I am a real-life Wonder Woman!

7

The Seventh Pillar of Power

THE POWER OF PERSPECTIVE

What Is Enough?

"Why am I never enough?" she asked. "I hate being me."

Those ugly words pierced straight through to my soul. I looked into my fourteen-year-old daughter's glistening eyes. I fought back the patronizing maternal clichés that wanted to tumble out of my mouth. Instead, I asked her a simple question.

"What is *enough*?"

She looked at me, perplexed and exhausted. She let out a long, deep breath, something between a shudder and a sigh. The light from her reading lamp reflected off her tear-stained cheeks as we sat on her bed, close enough to touch but not actually touching. I wanted to embrace her with every fiber of my being, but I knew she needed some space. So I calmly repeated the question.

"What is enough, honey? Who gets to deicide?"

She'd just told me about being brutally betrayed by a friend. She'd shared her innermost feelings of failure, self-judgment, imperfection. Feelings of being less than and not enough.

My daughter was broken. She needed my loving support.

She also needed to find perspective.

I knew I had to help her find some sort of solution to these feelings of inadequacy. But how?

We All Need Perspective

The Power of Perspective might just be the most important Pillar of Power. Without the Power of Perspective, it's difficult to tap into the Power of Resilience, Authenticity, Priority, Tribe, Grace, or Voice. So let's take some time to explore this key power, shall we? (Make yourself comfortable—it's a long chapter.)

You see, a lack of perspective is not exclusive to teenage girls. It's not limited to young people and certainly not limited to women. It's human to lose our perspective.

I do believe, however, that we women tend to question our value frequently, if not continuously, throughout life. I see it as I travel the country speaking to women on college campuses and in boardrooms. I hear it from baggage handlers and computer programmers, from students and CEOs.

Every day we see women—daughters, mothers, sisters, colleagues, friends—struggle to find perspective on this unattainable quest for perfection:

★ Tweens and teens comparing themselves to unrealistic images as the toxic quest for perfection takes root.

★ Young women crumbling under the pressure of career aspirations and expectations.

★ Moms exhausting themselves by trying to create a Pinterest-worthy lifestyle for their children.

★ Professional women striving to attain the perfect work-life balance (as if there were such a thing) and second-guessing themselves every step of the way.

★ Retired women seeking meaning and validation in this new season of life and feeling unfulfilled or less than.

At times, we each feel left out, less than, or not enough. We fail. We fall. We do our best.

But seriously, who gets to decide what *enough* is? How do we, as women, recognize when we are judging ourselves—or others—too harshly? Where do we find much-needed perspective?

Real-Life Wonder Women

In researching this chapter, not only did I read dozens of books and articles on perspective and transformation but I also connected with hundreds of real-life Wonder Women of all ages. I wanted to see if I could find a consensus in thoughts on perspective.

Their responses overwhelmed me and enlightened me. I had as many different responses as I did women. But in most responses, the word *perfection* came up as the thief of perspective.

Here is some of the wisdom these women shared:

Focus on the big picture. Once I do that, I look at life from a position that is all-encompassing. It's easy to find contentment, happiness, and be open to new experiences when you're not focused on perfection.

— BECCA, 38

As we mature, our perspective on perfection continues to change. Although I no longer strive to look like a runway model in my swimsuit, I do keep a neat and orderly house with freshly baked cookies awaiting my children's return home. I still strive for perfection in other areas of my life. I am not sure that that part will ever change. It is a continuing journey; however, I think I am better in dealing with it. Having good relationships—whether it be with my spouse, children, or close friends—helps me keep my perspective. We are human and we all deal with the same thought distortions at times. You don't have to be perfect to be loved, respected, and valued!

— SUSAN, 55

Perspective means learning how to better recognize the different aspects of my personality. In particular, I'm learning more about my inner critic. I'm starting to learn her tricks. She's loud and melodramatic. She claims she knows best and wants the best for me, yet she's full of fear and doubt. While I can't ignore her, I realize now that I don't have to believe her. I can choose to separate her from my decisions. Instead, I'm learning to listen carefully for my inner champion. She's quiet but sure. This is the part of me that is brave, hopeful, and grounded. She truly does know best. Perspective is learning how to empower her so she can empower me.

— ANGIE, 41

Perspective is something that affects my attitude, thoughts, and, frankly, my whole being each and every day. I strive to look at things positively and with as much gratitude as I can. But sometimes it is difficult to be the light when things seem so dark. Thoughts of perfection, failure, and judgment often run through my head and affect how I look at situations. That is where perspective can either make or break you. Choosing to look at the hardships and challenges in life with a softer edge and choosing to make a conscious effort to give myself more grace has made all the difference in the world for me.

—RACHAEL, 22

Work on you. Worry less about what others think and more about the positive change you can make in the world.

—ANNIE, 50

I believe I have a unique perspective because I am forty-eight, single, and childless. So what matters to me may not even hit the radar of another woman my age who is married, has children, and maybe even grandchildren. I think I can still have perspective, even though I want to be as "perfect" as I can be. Is one exclusive of the other? I don't think so. For me, it's not about keeping up with the Joneses—or what would they call it . . . Mrs. Jones? That is unattainable. I will always come up short comparing myself. Someone will always be younger, prettier, skinnier, have more money, a better car, etc. Sorry, I am not playing with that!

I can make choices that put my best self forward, whether that be on my outer or inner self. I can strive to be my best. Does that mean having a spray tan because it looks better with a sundress? Does that mean spending time journaling? Or walking my dogs, even in the rain, because they LOVE their walks? Or going to an exercise class because I know I'll feel better when I'm finished?

Instead of perfection being a dirty word, I'm going to make it a positive thing. I'm searching for MY perfection, and that's a good thing! I'm past worrying about what society wants perfection to look like on me. I determine what my perfect will be.

—LORI, 48

I work in information technology (IT). My colleagues would tell you that I often say, "Perfect is the enemy of good" and "Done is better than perfect." This isn't just fitting for IT but also for life. Perfection shouldn't be the constant goal. We lead full lives and need to be able to discern when "perfect" versus "good" or "done" is acceptable.

—JODY, 54

I think women need to remember that so much of how people respond to you is not about what you did or didn't do. It's about them—that they are empty, they are struggling, stressed, afraid that they are doing it all wrong. Our value lies inside of us. When we look to the world to fill us, we follow the roller coaster up and down. But when we are centered and when we understand our worth, the roller coaster of wanting the world to love us fades away. I have to remind myself almost daily that my value is within me. The world does not decide what I have to offer. I decide.

—KRIS, 43

Perspective is wisdom and humor. Enjoying your personality. Building capacity. One step at a time.

—CAROL, 65

We are constantly in comparison mode. Women are filled with insecurities! Every woman has a deep need for love. We are searching for love everywhere. We are missing the fact that we have one person who MUST love us, and that is ourselves! As nurturing creatures who can find it easy and natural to show love for someone else, isn't it amazing how hard it is for us to do this for ourselves? We must recognize truth and love, and live in our blessings. This is where perspective changes and perfection gets thrown out the window! Good riddance!

—JENNIFER, 34

Forget Perfection—Find Perspective

Do your thoughts align with any of these real-life Wonder Women? How do you feel about the idea of perfection? How can you overcome painful obstacles and comparisons and find a life of contentment and perspective?

Get Curious for the Truth

When feeling less than, ask yourself, *Is this the truth? Or is it the story I'm telling myself?* As humans, we often tweak the truth, then repeat these twisted versions of it in our heads. Sometimes others echo this "truth" back to us too.

Unfortunately, these kinds of comments can take up residence in our brains for years if we don't get curious, put them under the light, and then choose to block them. So it's time to give those stories a reality check. You get to decide which stories take up the valuable real estate in your head. You get to control your perspective.

My friend Annie had a rough start in life. Her family situation was less than ideal, and her childhood involved unfortunate cycles of neglect and abuse. She was malnourished, with her pants sometimes falling off her frail little body. In spite of this, her sisters nick-named her "Bubble Butt" and teased her about her body shape.

"In my head, I have always had a big butt, even when I didn't have one," Annie explains. "I've had to rewrite the story I tell myself and rerecord the tapes running in my head so the roadblocks are removed."

Jennifer, another real-life Wonder Woman I interviewed, believes perspective requires the ability to look at things from all viewpoints. To her, perspective is more fact-based.

"It means compiling the facts on why people believe the way they do, what made them come to that conclusion, and what is healthy or not healthy about that," she says. "Perspective makes you look at all angles, it makes you ask why and dig deeper, and it helps you see things clearer."

If you find it hard to get to the truth, imagine wrapping Wonder Woman's golden Lasso of Truth around yourself. Whenever someone is wrapped in the lasso, they are forced to tell the truth—to others and to themselves.

Get Naked

Finding perspective often requires peeling off the layers of fear, doubt, protection, and per-fection. It's about vulnerability—getting naked in the sense of removing armor and barriers.

For some, it's like removing heavy shoes of fear that keep you stuck in a rut. For others, it's like shedding a cloak of shame from a past mistake. What does it feel like for you? No matter what layer you need to remove, there's tremendous power and growth in stripping your fear and trusting your authentic self.

We have to allow ourselves to be seen. We must reveal our imperfections. We must have the courage to be vulnerable and the compassion to be kind to ourselves and to others. This is how we grow in our self-worth and ultimately find our power.

This may be a long and sometimes painful process. But learning to strip away the illusion of perfection will help you live a fuller, more authentic life. As Brené Brown states, "Owning our story and loving ourselves through the process is the bravest thing we'll ever do."

Trust Your Tribe

How do the people in your life help you keep perspective? Many women I spoke with rely on their tribe to help find and maintain perspective. We discussed tribe in chapter 4. These are the people who love and respect you enough to let you know when your perspective is skewed or when you need a reality check.

One young woman, age eighteen, who wished to remain anonymous, said, "I struggle with negative self-esteem. I can very easily get into a place of self-doubt, which can take on a life of its own, if not stopped. Fortunately, I have a close friend who is not afraid to call B.S. when she sees me start to tank. She doesn't mince words. She cares enough about me and my well-being to be honest. She knows just what to say and do to help me find perspective. I am lucky to have her as a friend."

Laura, an insurance executive, relies on her inner circle for clarity and perspective both personally and in her professional role. "The people closest to me recognize my strengths and also remind me that it is okay to take a step back, listen, and let things happen before making a decision and moving forward," she explained. "Plus, the older I get, the more willing I am to take in other perspectives and recognize them as a learning opportunity and not a threat to the way I think I want something to happen."

Observe, Don't Judge

The word *perspective* literally means the ability to view something from a particular angle. So if we want more perspective in our lives, we must learn to observe without judgment.

So how do you distinguish judgment from observation? A judgment is when we attach a feeling to an action or situation. We decide if it's "right" or "wrong," "good" or "bad." But when we observe, we simply witness what is occurring without attaching a feeling. It helps us accept the situation as is—without trying to control it or change it.

Observing our own life without judgment takes practice. It's not natural to step back and view a situation without emotion, to note nuances and details, but not to compare or label. It's challenging in real time and in real life. But it is doable.

For example, think about when we make a mistake. We tend to think, *I'm a complete failure.* We judge and label our person, as if that one action defines who we are. This leads us to shut down instead of work harder to remedy the situation.

The narrative of an observer might go something like this: *Hmm, that didn't go as I had hoped. I'm disappointed in the outcome. I may want to try again.* It still addresses the situation and even identifies some of the emotions associated with it. But it doesn't judge or label the person. There's a drive here to right the situation because we don't let it define us.

Do you see the difference?

It's time to change the narrative, my brave friends. It's okay to own your mistakes and not rush to judgment. You will persevere and evolve. You will learn from your mistakes and find power in perspective.

The Perspective Stick

If you're still wondering how I ultimately handled that situation with my daughter, I wish I could tell you that I immediately saved the day. That I was like Wonder Woman using her magical bracelets to shield this sweet girl from the evils of insecurity and doubt. That I blinded her with the power of perspective so she could feel secure and loved and accepted.

Believe me, I tried. I wrapped her in words of affirmation, praising her integrity and character. I gave hugs. Lots and lots of hugs. I held her close as we talked about seeking the truth—the real truth—about herself, not just some story percolating in her brain, telling her she wasn't enough. I reminded her that she was not alone, that we all feel angst at times. And that she would persevere.

She seemed to grasp the concepts, but she was exhausted. Emotionally and physically drained. Truth be told, so was I. So I tucked her in and sent up a short prayer. I asked for guidance in how to proceed, begging God to help her find peace and perspective.

I knew I needed to do more, but what? How could I help her remember her own value and worth? How could I help her keep perspective? Words, concepts, hugs, and prayers were all wonderful, but I knew I had to come up with something tangible—something she could literally *grasp*.

Then the idea hit me. I didn't have magic bracelets. But I could make a magic wand.

A perspective stick.

Now, before I go any further, you need to know I am not a crafty person. I can't sew. My scrapbooks look like they were designed by a first grader. But I had a glue gun and a mission.

So I dug out our box of fabric scraps (which we had only because my mom, a seamstress, left them for us). I proceeded to glue some furry white fabric onto an old, beat-up ruler. I trimmed the ends with some hot-pink felt and a ribbon imprinted with the words *laugh-live-happy-love-smile* in rainbow colors.

"What's this?" she asked when I presented it to her the next morning.

"It's a perspective stick," I said.

"A what?" she asked, clearly confused.

"It's like a magic wand," I explained. "It will remind you to give yourself some grace and to seek truth and perspective. All you have to do is to tap yourself on the head with it. I'd be happy to whack you with it once in a while," I added with a wink for some levity.

She smiled. Then she took the perspective stick and gave it a test run, tapping herself on the forehead.

"I think it's working already," she said. "Thanks, Mom . . . for everything."

Let's fast-forward several years to her college move-in day. I was a mess. I was excited for her to embark on this new adventure. I was also terrified to let her go. After eighteen years of pouring my heart and soul into raising this young human, how could I just plop her down on a college campus, walk away, and expect her to survive?

We were helping her unpack two carloads of belongings into her tiny dorm room. I was folding towels and fighting back tears when I felt something tap me on the back of the head.

"You look like you need some perspective, Mom."

And that's when I understood the true magic of the perspective stick. Perspective is a superpower, yes, but one that inevitably comes and goes through every twist and turn of life. It isn't a constant. And sometimes all it takes is a fabric-covered ruler to help us gain what we've lost, reclaim what we've given away, and remember what we've forgotten.

With a knowing smile, my daughter then placed the perspective stick on the headboard of her bed so she'd see it every day.

The power of perspective.

Wonder-Full.

What is enough? *Who* gets to deicide?

The answer is *you*.

YOU get to decide what is enough.

YOU get to choose the stories you tell yourself, so make sure they are actually true.

YOU get to remove barriers, set healthy boundaries, and trust your authentic self.

YOU get to define you—brave, beautiful, powerful, Wonder-Full you.

YOU get to find power in perspective.

And that is something to celebrate.

What does perspective mean to you?

THOUGHTBOOK

Final Words of Wonder

Friends, let's unite as brave, Wonder-Full women! Let's change how we look at each other. Let's identify one another's superpowers and celebrate them, instead of comparing or judging.

Let's change how we look at ourselves too. What are *your* superpowers? What kind of Wonder Woman are *you*? As we near the end of this book, I urge you to take a moment to discover just how Wonder-Full you are.

Indeed, you can live a life of abundance. In addition to your own unique gifts, you now have the Seven Pillars of Power to provide structure and guidance. You can start—today, right this moment—by choosing to:

★ Bounce back after a fall and become more resilient

★ Live an authentic life and influence people in a bolder, more positive way

★ Do less better so you can be more present

★ Surround yourself with people who motivate you to be better

★ Be gracious and kind to yourself and others

★ Empower with affirmative words

★ Forget perfection and find perspective

My friends, please remember that you are strong and smart and compassionate.

You have the power to lead.

To mentor.

To love.

To conquer fears and overcome challenges.

So lift up your sisters and enlist your tribe. Activate your superpowers. Celebrate your authentic self and live a Wonder-Full life.

No cape required.

We all have superpowers within us! By now, you've probably realized that "superpowers" are Wonder Woman talk for "character qualities." Some superpowers are present from birth, but many are learned throughout life.

It is often easy to identify others' superpowers but more challenging to identify our own. But we must identify them, own them, and channel them for greater good.

When you turn the page, you'll see a list of superpowers. It's not a comprehensive list by any means. There are many more! But it's a place to start. Scan the list and think about your own character qualities. Do certain words jump out at you? If you especially struggle here, ask your tribe members to describe you in three words.

So, what are *your* superpowers? List three below.

Now that you've identified some of your superpowers, take a few moments to think about how you are currently using them.

Are you using your superpowers to make a difference? At home? At work? At school? Are you using your powers for greater good? To improve the lives of others? How are you using your powers to support the women in your tribe? What would Wonder Woman do (#WWWWD) if she possessed your particular superpowers? What can you start doing today to share your powers with others?

Finally, it's time to become a superhero and take action! Below you will see three "I will" statements. Write down three tangible, doable actions you can—and will—take in the next seven days to use your superpowers for greater good. Nothing is too big or too small.

I will _____

_____

I will _____

_____

I will _____

_____

Read these sentences aloud, then add: "I am Wonder-Full!"

ADAPTABLE	DEVOTED	HELPFUL	RELIABLE
ADVENTUROUS	DILIGENT	HONEST	RESILIENT
AMBITIOUS	DISCIPLINED	HUMBLE	RESPECTFUL
APPRECIATIVE	EAGER	HUMOROUS	RESPONSIBLE
APPROACHABLE	EASYGOING	IMAGINATIVE	SELF-CONFIDENT
ARTISTIC	ENCOURAGING	INDEPENDENT	SINCERE
BRAVE	ENERGETIC	INSPIRING	SMART
BRIGHT	ENTHUSIASTIC	INTELLIGENT	SPIRITUAL
BRILLIANT	FAIR	JOYFUL	STRONG
CALM	FAITHFUL	LOGICAL	STUDIOUS
CANDID	FORGIVING	LOVABLE	SUCCESSFUL
CARING	FRIENDLY	LOVING	TALENTED
CHEERFUL	FUN-LOVING	LOYAL	THOUGHTFUL
COMPASSIONATE	FUNNY	MATURE	TOLERANT
CONSCIENTIOUS	GENEROUS	OBSERVANT	TRUSTWORTHY
CONSIDERATE	GENTLE	OPTIMISTIC	UNIQUE
COOPERATIVE	GIVING	PASSIONATE	UNSELFISH
COURAGEOUS	GRACIOUS	PATIENT	WARM
CREATIVE	GRATEFUL	PERCEPTIVE	WISE
CURIOUS	GRITTY	PERSISTENT	WITTY
DEPENDABLE	HAPPY	POSITIVE	
DETERMINED	HARDWORKING	PROFICIENT	

Acknowledgments

In my opinion, this just might be the most important section of the book. It's where I get to thank the many people who shared their superpowers to make this book a reality. It's with heartfelt gratitude that I recognize the following:

My tribe—you know who you are. You are fierce! You push me to be better. You inspire me and bring color, depth, and joy to my world. You are simply Wonder-Full.

The real-life Wonder Women—thank you for allowing me to feature you and interview you for my book and my blog. You have courage. It is because of your authenticity and generosity that this book is even possible.

Karen and Brooke—you are two of the strongest, bravest women I know. Thank you for allowing me to share our stories and life lessons. And, of course, thank you for the Wonder Woman lunchbox. I am proud to be your mom.

Marty—you are my hero and the love of my life. Thank you for believing in me even before I began to believe in myself. I adore you.

Lynda Carter—for bringing Wonder Woman to life. You taught ten-year-old me that women could have fierce strength, kind hearts, and incredible valor.

My childhood neighbor, Jodi—thanks for sharing my affinity for Wonder Woman when we were little girls. I still remember how we'd wear Wonder Woman Underoos (yes, the underwear that's fun to wear) and run through our backyards, saving the world from evil. Apparently, that's what kids did before iPads. #goodtimes

Lily and the Pond crew at Beaver's Pond Press—thanks for keeping me organized, on track, and sane. You make publishing fun!

Athena—when I first heard your name, I knew you were the woman for this project. *A woman named Athena? With a degree in illustrating comics?* You can't make this up! You wow me with your talent.

Angie, my editor extraordinaire—you are and always will be the Queen of Transitions. Your enthusiasm for this book brought it to life. Thank you for your patience, guidance, and grace.

Jennifer Strunk, proofreader—thank you for your supersharp eyes and amazing attention to detail. You are a wording wizard!

My professional speaking colleagues and mentors at the Minnesota chapter of the National Speakers Association—I am grateful for your support and insight.

My spectacular clients—thank you for inviting me to share my stories, research, and nuggets of wisdom to empower your teams, students, colleagues, and staff. Because of you, I love what I do!

You, the reader—thank you for investing in this book. You are the reason I write. You give me energy, motivation, and validation. I am honored to serve you and eager to learn how you use your superpowers to bring positive energy to the people you encounter.

And finally, to God—you gave me the passion, the drive, the words, the people, and the superpowers to make this all happen. Glory be to you!

About the Author

Kelly Radi is a real-life Wonder Woman! She's a sought-after speaker, award-winning author, and CEO of Radi to Write, LLC.

Authentic, inspiring, and relatable, Kelly equips and empowers her audiences to find—and use—their unique inner superpowers to live Wonder-Full lives.

A member of the National Speakers Association, Kelly earned the 2018 NSA Minnesota Speaker Academy Award.

Kelly lives in Minnesota with her husband, Marty. She likes reading, red wine, Southern rock, things that sparkle, and watching her daughters learn to "adult." And yes, she has a thing for Wonder Woman.

Learn more about Kelly at raditowrite.com.

Kelly Radi

Hire Kelly to Speak

Kelly validates and connects with her audience by intertwining real stories, superhero history lessons, and relevant takeaways. Her heartfelt delivery inspires people to take personal accountability, act with integrity, and develop stronger relationships, so they can create a life of significance—both personally and professionally.

After all, superheroes don't just sit there. They take action!

If you are interested in bringing Kelly Radi to your company, organization, or school for a conference or workshop, please contact her through her website at raditowrite.com.

Kelly Radi is truly a Wonder Woman! She teaches with storytelling that makes you smile. She inspires with passion. You leave her session ready to go out and make a difference. Now, where's my cape?

—ALLISON LENSINK, DELTA AIR LINES

Kelly is so authentic in her experiences, her struggles and her victories. She speaks to your heart because she is speaking from her heart.

—KRIS NELSON, PREMIER REAL ESTATE

Booking Kelly to speak is a sure way to motivate your attendees to take action when they leave. Her message was extremely well received at our conference and had a profound impact on the women in attendance.

—MICHELLE PAPE, CEO NEXT MONDAY

Also by Kelly Radi

All aboard, parents! It's time to see your child off on the voyage of a lifetime: the first year of college. This transition can be stressful and emotional. How do parents survive back on shore when they send their child out to sea?

Never fear—here is your survival guide! *Out to Sea* will help you navigate the emotional and practical aspects of the freshman year with real-world advice from parents and experts alike.

Ensure smoother sailing with tips on:

- Packing—with handy checklists
- Staying connected
- Mentorship parenting
- Money matters
- Academic expectations
- Roommate relations
- Health and wellness
- What to expect when your student comes home
- And more!

outtoseaparentsguide.com